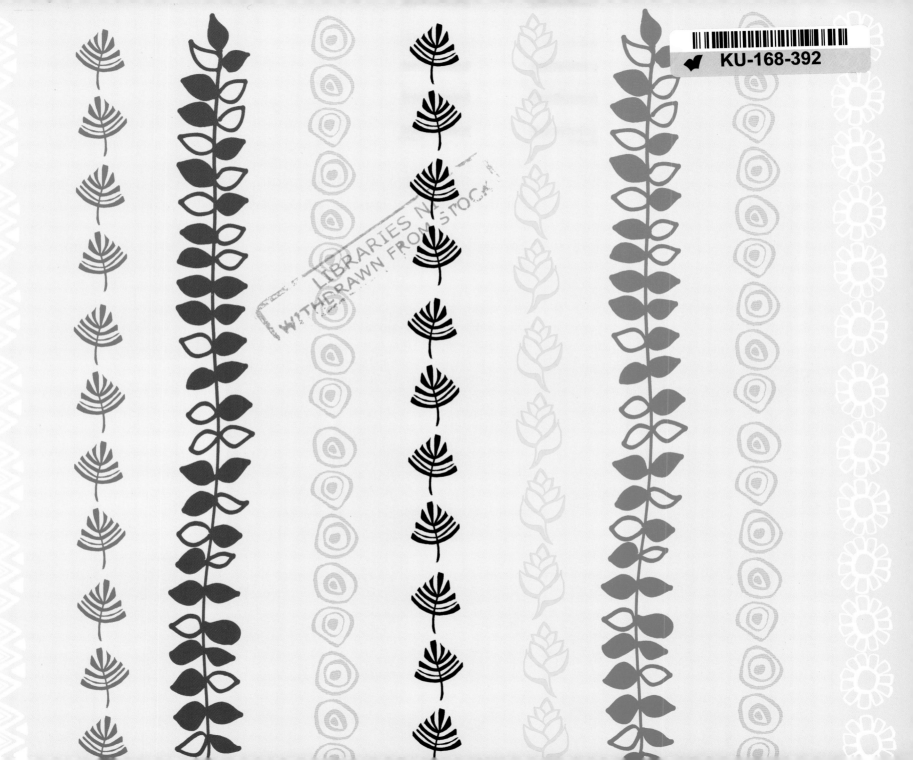

For my mum. She made me a little bit Jamaican – B.Z.
For the children of Jamaica – P.D.

The Author, Photographer and Publisher would like to thank
Claire Barry, Horace Forbes, Louise Moore, The National Library of Jamaica,
Jackie and Emma Ranston, Renford Taylor of the Jamaica Union of Travellers
Association (JUTA), Kerr Thompson, and Donna and Philip Wilson
for helping to make this book possible.

First published in Great Britain and in the USA in 2006
by Frances Lincoln Children's Books, 4 Torriano Mews,
Torriano Avenue, London NW5 2RZ

First paperback edition published in Great Britain in 2009

www.franceslincoln.com

British Library Cataloguing in Publication Data available on request

ISBN 978-1-84507-609-2

Printed in China

1 3 5 7 9 8 6 4 2

J is for Jamaica

Benjamin Zephaniah

Prodeepta Das

F

FRANCES LINCOLN
CHILDREN'S BOOKS

Author's note

Jamaica is a small island in the Caribbean
Sea, but the influence of its music, literature
and fashion can be seen all over the world.
I was born in Birmingham, England but my
family come from St. Elizabeth, Jamaica and
I visit there almost every year. It is impossible
to talk about Jamaica without acknowledging
its problems, but every time I go there
I am amazed at how the people are able
to stay strong and offer a smile. It doesn't
matter how poor a person is, they are
always willing to share a mango or a fruit
juice with you. So I want to celebrate
a small island with a big heart, a place that
pulsates to music, a place where, if you wait
long enough, fruit will fall from a tree
to feed you. This is Jamaica.

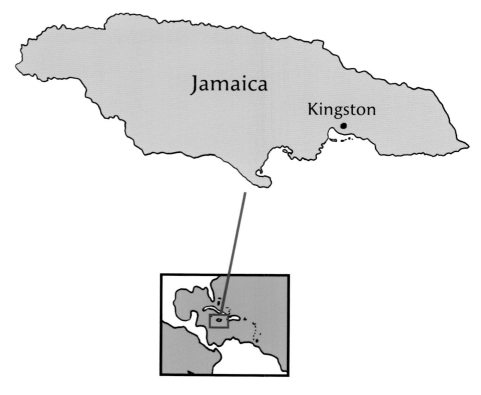

Aa

is for Ackee – yellow, soft, and nice,
They say if you eat ackee once you'll want to eat it twice.
It's a fruit and a vegetable, both savoury and sweet,
A symbol of Jamaica with a taste that is unique.

Bb

is for Blue Mountain, its beauty must be seen.
The lovely Blue Mountain is really very green.
In the centre of Jamaica, it rises to the sky,
And it looks very special when a rainbow passes by.

 is for Cricket – cricket, lovely cricket.
The bowler bowls the ball, the batter guards the wicket,
But the batters must be careful to protect their heads and knees.
The best players from Jamaica can play for the West Indies.

Dd

is for Dollars, Jamaica's currency,
And every adult must work hard to earn spending money.
A long time ago they used pounds, shillings and pence,
But now to make a dollar, you need a hundred cents.

 is for Education, and education is for all,
With knowledge and understanding Jamaicans can walk tall.
All children can go to a school where they can concentrate,
They know that clever children will make sweet Jamaica great.

F f is for Folklore, the stories people tell.
Some people say they are so real the stories have a smell.
Some stories make you happy, some make you shed some tears,
Still folklore has been part of life for many, many years.

 is for Goats, you can see them everywhere,
On the streets and beaches, you will see goats there.
Goats are very friendly, but it is worthwhile knowing,
They eat flowers, fruits, and plants – and anything that's growing.

H h

is for Hummingbird. This bird is small but clever,
It can hover in the sky no matter what the weather.
Its beak is long and thin to help it feed from trees,
It's seen around the flowers,
                              but it doesn't seem to sneeze.

I i

is for Irish Moss, a drink made from seaweed.
It's full of vitamins that every healthy body needs.
It's thick and sweet and slimy, a bit like a milkshake,
But if you want it to taste good,
                              it takes some skill to make.

 is for Jamaica, where the sun shines all year round.
Here waterfalls and mountains and beaches can be found.
The island is a place where many tourists like to be,
On the map you'll see it smiling in the Caribbean sea.

 is for Kingston, Jamaica's capital,
The biggest city in the land, it's just incredible!
So many people live here, everywhere there is a crowd,
And the buses and the market make the city very loud.

 is for Lizards, they're silent with no scent.

Some live in trees, some live indoors and lizards pay no rent.

Most people just ignore them, they're treated like insiders,

Some people think they're cleaners — because they eat the spiders.

 is for Markets – here things are bought and sold.
The vegetables are very fresh and lovely to behold.
The sellers sing their bargains and the buyers pay the price,
And even if you do not buy, just going can be nice.

 is for Netball – the game girls love to play.
Somewhere on this island this game's played every day.
Jamaicans love their netball as well as their athletics,
And that is why they send a netball team to the Olympics.

is for *One Love*, Jamaica's favourite motto.
You'll see it and you'll hear it everywhere that you go.
It means it doesn't matter who you are or where you're from,
In Jamaica there's a special sort of love for everyone.

 is for Pumpkin. Some people boil and bake them.
Some people put them in hot soups,
                    some people like to grate them.
And when the pumpkin's cooking on a fire in a pot,
Some people like to add pepper to make it really hot.

Qq

is for Quickstick, with pretty little flowers.
They grow so quick, plant a stick and they will grow in hours,
And very soon you'll see a tree growing very high.
It's great to see the quick Quickstick high up in the sky.

Rr

is for Rainforest, where many plants grow,
The amount of wild plants growing is impossible to know.
The whole world needs rainforests, they grow when it is raining,
Some of them have been destroyed, that's why
                                    the climate's changing.

Ss

is for Sugar Cane – cane juice is very sweet.
The cane is very nice when sucked but difficult to eat.
That is why they crush the cane in busy factories,
And that is how they get sugar for all our cups of teas.

Tt is for Tamarind, they make sweets, and drinks, and sauces.
Some large meals have got tamarind somewhere in all the courses.
Grown high on the majestic tree with hot earth underneath –
The shell is hard, the pulp is soft, the seeds can break your teeth.

is for Ugli fruit, but is it really ugly?
It is a very special fruit and many think it's lovely.
A cross between a grapefruit and a tangerine,
It isn't really ugly, it's pretty and it's green.

 is for Veranda, where people talk and rest.
Most households have a veranda to entertain their guest,
A place to sit and eat and drink and shelter from the sun,
A place to sing and tell stories, and have a bit of fun.

is for Waterlilies – the water is their home.
There are so many of them, they never grow alone.
The lilies of the water are so small and light they float,
But sometimes they are pushed aside when there is a boat.

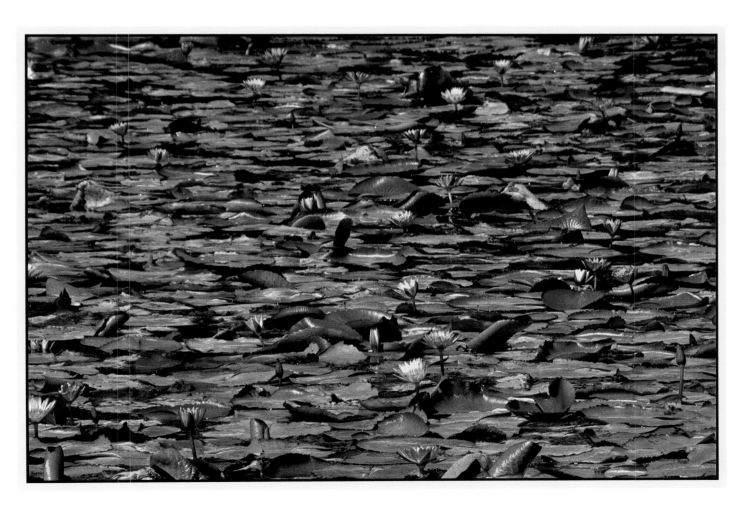

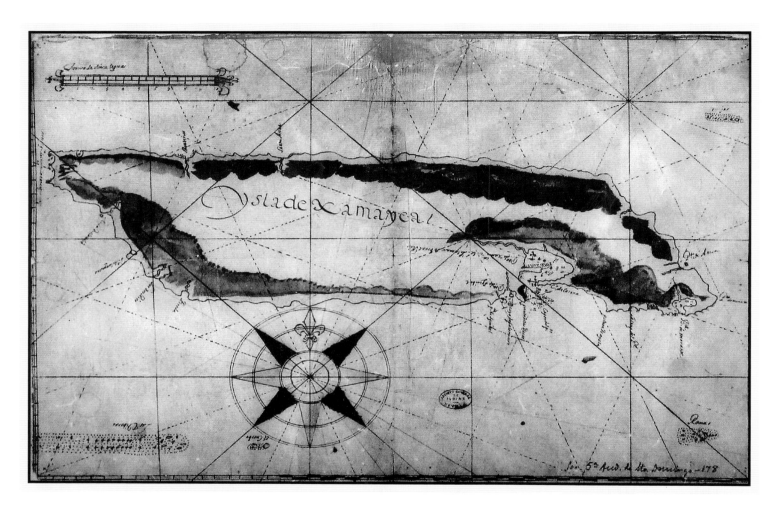

 is for Xamayca, one of the first names for Jamaica.
This tropical island can be found just south of the Equator.
It was also called Hamaika, Xaymaica and Santiago,
And going back a long time it was called a big volcano!

is for Yams, which are grown in the ground,
They are light and dark and long and round.
They're boiled in salt water on a medium heat,
And in fifteen minutes, they're ready to eat.

is for Zinc roof – now stop a while and think –
Not all the zinc roofs you will see are really made of zinc.
They're made of many metals, there is a wide selection.
They're cheap, and when there's nothing else,
                              they offer you protection.

MORE PICTURE BOOKS IN THE WORLD ALPHABET SERIES
FROM FRANCES LINCOLN CHILDREN'S BOOKS

B is for Brazil
Maria de Fatima Campos

From the wilds of the Amazon rain forest to the busy streets of São Paulo, from Carnival to Jangada; from football to Zebu cattle – *B is for Brazil* shows this lively South American country in all its colourful diversity. Maria de Fatima Campos's full-colour photographs capture the essence of Brazilian life - the interweaving of its cultures and peoples - as she leads the reader on an alphabetic tour.

C is for China
Sungwan So

From Abacus to Lantern, from Jade to Wenzi, here is a stunning photographic book, capturing the rhythms of day-to-day life in China. Sungwan So's evocative photographs combine with simple, informative text to present a colourful portrait of Chinese culture, craft and custom. Informative, enlightening and entertaining.

W is for World
Kathryn Cave
In association with Oxfam

From Alfredo in Mozambique to Zoe in Jamaica, take a glimpse at the lives of children across the globe in this photographic alphabet book. Featuring over 20 countries from Greenland to Vietnam, it shows how many things people of different backgrounds have in common.

Frances Lincoln titles are available from all good bookshops.
You can also buy books and find out more about your favourite titles,
authors and illustrators on our website: www.franceslincoln.com